21 Shades of Being

Vesper Grace

BookLeaf
Publishing

India | USA | UK

Presentation by *BookLeaf Publishing*

Web: www.bookleafpub.com

E-mail: info@bookleafpub.com

ISBN: 9789360946166

First edition 2024

*To my Mother, whose love held me steady
through life's storms.*

This voyage is a tribute to yours.

ACKNOWLEDGEMENT

To my dearest Ankit Choudhary and Gauri Pendsay,

I express my deep sense of gratitude for your constant attention to detail. From finalizing the perfect name to finding the ideal colors for the book cover, your contributions were invaluable. You pushed me forward every day throughout the writing journey, acting as both my critic and my motivator. Thank you for your unwavering support.

To Aainee Sheikh and Hiteshwar Reddy,

Thank you for lending a listening ear to my stories and for helping me with the author's page. Your support means a lot.

To my brother, Saurav Raj,

Your excitement for this project from day one fueled my motivation. Your willingness to discuss the emotional depth of my work and your unwavering support throughout this journey is something I am so grateful for.

To my childhood buddies, Smruti Rekha, Ankita Mahapatro, and Saurav Choudhary,

Thank you for recognizing and validating my talent when I couldn't see it myself. Your belief in me has been instrumental in my growth as a writer.

To Rohit Singh,

I am grateful for all the storytelling you did. You shared ideas that became sources of inspiration for my poems, and our conversations helped me navigate creative roadblocks.

Finally,

To the lovers who taught me the depths of love and to the friends whose paths diverged from mine—thank you for crossing paths. Each encounter, both cherished and poignant, has shaped me in profound ways.

PREFACE

The dream of becoming an author sprouted within me at the tender age of fourteen. We are, after all, shaped by the experiences, choices, and currents of life that carry us along. Witnessing my Mama craft beautiful *shayaris* and my Baba's love for books instilled within me a deep love for the written word. Perhaps it was the limited technology of my youth, but solace found me nestled within the pages of countless stories. A burning desire ignited—to create something that could hold the same power for others.

"Paper has more patience than people," Anne Frank once wrote. These words resonated deeply, reflecting a truth I felt instinctively. As a teenager, the world sometimes felt overwhelming, and expressing myself authentically seemed daunting. But within the quiet space of a notebook, I found a safe haven, a confidante who held my thoughts and feelings with unwavering patience. This is why I started writing—to capture the kalcidoscope of emotions within and explore the depths of the human experience.

Then, unexpectedly, the opportunity blossomed. This book, a chance encounter with destiny, presented itself as a challenge—a chance to fulfill a lifelong dream. The journey of crafting these poems became an exploration of the self. I delved into the well of memory, revisiting past emotions to capture their essence with the keen eye of a listener and observer. This process, of unearthing and expressing, has been one of the most enriching experiences of my life.

21 Shades of Being is a vibrant constellation of emotions, not just my own, but a reflection of the human experience shared by those around me.

It is a celebration of life, dedicated to those who dared to love, endured loss, navigated the depths of heartbreak and trauma, and yet chose to live.

Let these poems wash over you, a balm for the soul's many shades. Turn the page and embark on a journey of the heart.

**Perhaps within these verses, you'll see a piece of yourself, a reflection of your own

experience, a familiar feeling, or a moment of comfort.

If your journey has mirrored any of these hardships, and yet you chose to fight, to live—then know this: you are braver than you know.

Open these pages and discover the strength within your own 21 shades of being.

Beneath

In the shadows
We learn to hide
Burying true emotions, deep inside
Unseen, unspoken
Longing for acceptance
For in their Rawness
Love is denied.

Good girls paint on smiles
Boys choke back tears
Suppressing Pain, Masking fears
But behind closed doors,
In solitude's sears,
Sobs echo,
Unbidden,
Like haunting Souvenirs.

Perhaps
Love me less,
Love me wild,
In winter's embrace,
Like a lost child.

In the night, In silence
On darkest days

Hold me tight
Embrace my mess

Let love be,
A gentle touch

A bit less perfect,
Yet just as much,
A bit less perfect,
Yet just as much.

She tries

She breaks, She hurts
She runs away, she loves
She accepts, she avoids
She fails, she tries...

She is scared, she knows
Tell her to give up,
She won't
Offer help, she denies
She fails, she tries...

She is fierce, she's wise
When no one's watching
She often cries
With every stumble,
She learns to rise
She fails, she tries...

For she is more than tears and sighs
With every challenge, she testifies
In depths of courage, she contrives
Even with the toughest trials
She survives...

Overthinking

It's haunted in here
There's a lot of noise coming in
The demons, they are loud.
They scream

I feed them,
I wait,
I wait for them to go to sleep
Creepy creatures lurk around
And watch me when I weep
They don't escape
They don't flee
They stay by my side
A constant companion in the tumultuous ride.
But sometimes I grow weary
Sick of their taunt
Their words like poison
Leaving me gaunt.

I try to break free,
To leave them behind
But they find me again
In the recesses of my mind.

Dilemma

The call of two worlds
Echoes in my soul
One whispers comfort
The other makes me whole
In childhood's haven, a sanctuary of memories
Familiar scents, sheets
Every corner of the town
Carries beautiful stories...

Yet, wanderlust beckons,
With a vibrant hum
To fly to unknown distant lands
Where I don't belong
Before life becomes numb

But time, a tyrant, rations out the days
Leaving me stranded in a glided maze
Choices I make have constant burning cost
Increasing the void, with every moment lost.

I search for balance
In the endless fight
To chase the sunrise while holding on to the
night.

The conflict rages,
A constant ebb and flow
Where to find solace, where my spirit can grow?
Can both flames coexist in this heart so torn?
Or must I choose,
And leave one side to mourn?

Coz,
Home's a feeling I hold,
And not just a place
My soul seeks for both
The comfort and the chase.

My soul seeks for both
The comfort and the chase.

Depression

I want to go out
And be out there
It's just that I can't
You ask me why?
I have no clue…
Never really thought
Getting up would be so hard
That it would make no sense
And drive me mad
You ask me the reason??
I wish I knew…
It looks so easy, right?
But I just can't do
What's wrong with me?
I wish I knew…
I try to understand
I miserably fail
Nothing makes sense to me
Everything looks pale
You ask me if I am alright?
I pause
I stare
Fine, Am I?
Well, I have no clue…

Fearless

She stood there
Unbothered,
A statue in the inferno's heart,
While the world around her sputtered,
Consumed by the fiery work of art.
Burning,
A forest caught in pain,
Yet in her eyes,
No flicker of dismay,
As if the flames were just her domain,
The first flame, born on that very day.

Her laughter, a crackling counterpoint,
Mocked the world's pathetic charade.
The heat licked hungrily, joint by joint,
But she stood firm, a monument unfazed.
This destruction, a furious heartstart
Pulled at the world, tearing it apart.

Then, with a final, earsplitting boom,
The inferno reached crescendo's height.
The world dissolved, consumed in the gloom,
Leaving behind only ash and fading light.

She stood alone,

like a silhouette stark,
Against the dawn's first,
tentative rays.
No triumph shone, no victory's mark,
Just a wasteland whispering in the haze.

The once vibrant forest, a smoldering pyre,
Mirrored the emptiness etched in her soul.
The firestorm's fury, a searing desire,
Had consumed all, leaving her cold and whole.

No tears fell,
no cries pierced the air,
Just a chilling vacant stare.
The world she knew, reduced to ash and despair,
A destruction beyond compare.

She took a step,
her form rippling and frail,
Embers danced where her feet left their trace.
The victor unclaimed, in this desolate trail,
A queen in the ruins with a fireborn face.

Detour

Down the winding paths
Unsure & Green
I took a Wrong turn, Unseen
Between
"Was this the way?"
My mind did fret,
Each twist & turn,
Looked like a threat
"Wrong turn!" It screamed.

Bad date, bad job, a series of woes,
The path I once wanted seemed covered in
throes.
Packed up my bags with a tear and a sigh,
Moved to a new city,
To give it another try.

Turns out, the "wrong turn" wasn't a plight,
Led to friendships that bloomed, shining ever so
bright.

The wrong turns,
They taught me to trust and believe,
That happiness waits, just around the next
sleeve.

The wrong turns,
They taught me to savor the now,
Not just the destination, but the journey,
somehow.

So let your heart wander, with an open mind's
view,
For sometimes the detours lead you to
something new.

Believe

Look around, so much to learn
Don't be afraid
You are not alone.

Believe in the process
Even with little progress
Believe in yourself
Like you believe on a window seat
For your every flight
While the afternoon view
Is not as amazing as the morning sight…

So, what's making you happy?
The joy of watching the view
Or the Joy of having the window seat to
yourself?
Coz having the window
It keeps you open to surprises you might get
You still cling to hope
And you are open to good fate
If you could love the window seat so much
You can love yourself a little bit too
If you can put your faith
On an hour-long flight
You can put your faith in life too

Some days would be way too blue

Some days could be way too cheerful
Some days could be dull
U might not get everything at once
You might get it all

Possibilities are endless
Don't miss out on your chance
Due to a lack of faith

Let belief be your driving force
Before it's too late.

Emptiness

Have you felt this too?

There's nothing wrong
But just isn't the usual "you?"
Not sad, not mad,
Just stuck in neutral, sailing slowly,
Not heartbroken, not angry
Just existing, with a gray inner light
Not complaining, not in a fiery rage
Just an empty feeling on life's empty stage
Not sobbing messy,
Not yelling at the wall
Just a hollow echo, barely there at all.

Living paradox

A rose's kiss, a velvet touch
Can leave you charmed or wounded much

A lover's presence, a tender hold
Can build your world or leave you cold

In hands that heal, a poison lies
The paradox of life, within our eyes

Kind words can heal like gentle rain
Harsh ones sting and leave agonizing pain

Sugar so sweet, a fleeting pleasure
Can give disease, a harsh measure

Knowledge, a tool of sharpest steel
Can build or break for good or ill
Fire provides both heat and light
But uncontrolled, it destroys every bit

The villain's mask, the hero's face
Both dance within the human space
So question, not the heavens above
For we are both the storm and the calm sea
Forever bound,

Eternally free

We hold the power to choose
To heal or harm, to win or lose
Right and wrong, they dance in time
But actions shape the future's rhyme

No God, no devil holds the key
Just us and what we choose to be.
Just us and what we choose to be.

Yearning

I want to live in fragments
Eternal & Endless
Like Multiple universes
Infinite & Boundless

Perhaps, then
I could be everywhere
Be a part of everything I desire
Have it all
That I hold dear

There's so much I wanna be
A little girl who's carefree
A pampered daughter
A passionate lover
A go-to friend to my peer
To hold everyone near
Like many branches of an old tree
To be with all
And to be able to rest guilt-free.

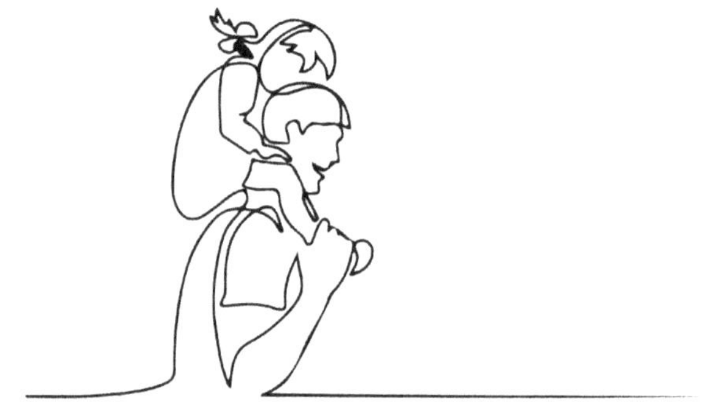

Lost

How would it be to top the school and run back
for your Dad, who is cheering for you?
How would it be to move to a new city without
any fear
Because Dad had said
Don't worry, my girl
I am here

How would it be to get a call from him
And ask how his little girl is adulting?

How would it be to enjoy the freedom away
from home, truly and happily, without any guilt;
Not worry about how lonely back at home your
Mom would be?

How would it be to see your parents cheer when
you win your every fear?

Why wasn't life fair to me?
Unlike everybody around me…
Why did not I get to live my happy life share?
Why was life so unfair??

With time everything heals, they say
Or with passing time you learn to be okay
It's been years now
There's this void I have tried to fill

I have tried my best
But the child who lost carries the pain in her
chest
With every passing year
All her special moments still feel undone
Like melodies missing their final perfect run

When you look around, there's so much to feel
That child could never really heal

Because
Some wounds leave scars that last through life's
race,
Each mark
A story of courage and Grace.

Loneliness

Underneath the Canopy
Of a start-studded sky
I lay bare my soul
Where my hidden feelings lie
With every pulsing beat
My heart longs to be heard
It speaks in silence
Without uttering a word
The storm raging within
Is a clash of hope and despair
The battle inside
Is a feeling I cannot share
It's a silent predator
It devours every thought
Leaving behind a void
Where pain is all I have got
The memories like shards of glass
Pierce through the dark
As I navigate the wreckage
Of a shattered heart.
No solace in the stars
No comfort in the moon
Just the emptiness of silence
An eternal gloom.

Holding On

It's gonna be hard
But let it go
Like that 3-year-old sweatshirt
I know I know
You kept it near the entire night
The day you got it
But now it just won't fit.
It's just lying there
Unworn
Untouched
Unloved, Just like you…

Let him go
I know I know
How he gave you butterflies
When both of you met
How every day felt like a date.

The stiff sweatshirt
It used to be your go-to hug,
Now scratchy fabric, an unwanted rug.

He feels the same, you have to face,
The love's worn thin into a faded space.

Those butterflies? Flew out the door,
Replaced by sighs you can't ignore.
You hold on tight, but deep inside,
A tiny voice whispers, "Let it slide."
You fight the urge to text him "Hey,"
But all you get back is "K" all day.

Let go of the old
Make a fresh start
Perhaps healing takes
A piece of your heart.

Him

He is strong
He is kind
Tells no one
What he feels inside.

Forces a quick laugh
To mask it all
Will clench his fists tight
But won't let tears fall

He acts tough
He hides his doubts
In a quiet place
He sometimes cries, sometimes shouts

Has built a wall to hide what stings
He pushes on with hidden wings.

Bricks he stacked
So high they reach
Maybe someday he will find his speech

May be someday
He will let love try
To peek behind the guided door

To see through the fake smile
What's hidden more.

Intuition

Lost in a puzzle of thoughts all blur
Stuck on a loop,
Completely unsure.

Logic keeps shouting
Like a tangled-up mess
Then you hear a whisper with a gentle caress.

It doesn't speak loudly
But nudges with care
Like a compass within you
Guiding you somewhere

Your mind tries logic
With a constant refrain
But the answer you seek
It can't quite explain

Listen up closely
To the voice within
It's stronger than the worries
Your mind can spin

So
Gut or Mind

Who is a friend?
Who is a foe?
Trust me
You will know

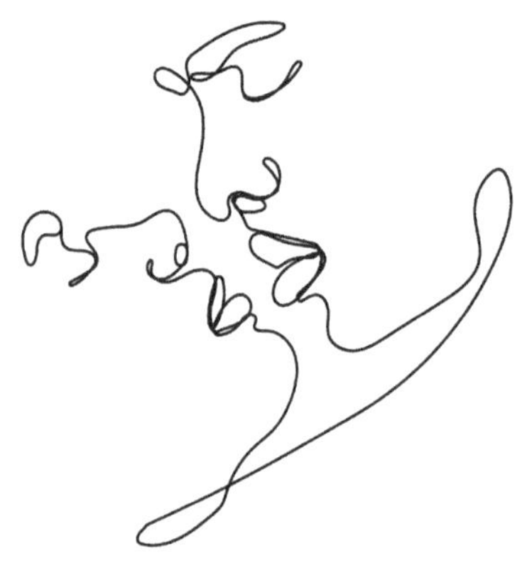

Intimacy

He traced his tongue
On my bare skin
Exploring every detail
Each raised valley
Every sunken dell.

His lips
A searing brand on every scar
A memorized landscape
Near and Far
Yet
In this Atlas
A truth remains untold
The deepest Canyon
My heart remains cold.

His kisses lingered
On the skin
An ephemeral spark
left the well of longing
Still so dark.

We were explorers
Hand in hand
Unraveling flesh

A foreign land
But in the caverns where shadows reside
Our souls remained strangers,
though entwined.
The irony is a bitter sting
Knowing every crevice
Yet nothing to cling

For intimacy transcends the body's thrall
To touch the bare skin was the easiest of all.

Unspoken

The clock ticks heavy
A metronome of woe
This night
A thief of hours refuses to go
The bed we shared
Now holds a cold space
A chilling reminder of an absent embrace
In this lonely room
I find myself wondering

Do unspoken feelings ever take flight?
Or do they fester in the lonely night?
Can a love story bloom without a sound,
Untethered to confessions, forever unbound?

Is love a melody the heart can't express
An eternal silence destined for distress?

Days turn to weeks, a chasm ever wide
Does unspoken love wither deep inside?

In the hushed silence
The answer chills my core
Would you ever miss me?
Would you ever love me more?

But a deeper terror grips my trembling soul
Will you ever know the love that took its toll?

If I dared to speak
What words would I say?
Would they chase love away
Or light the way?

Is the risk of rejection
Worse than the pain
Of a love unspoken
Forever in vain?

These questions echo
A cacophony of despair,
A love unspoken
A love I could not share.

Perhaps love unspoken is the cruelest art
A masterpiece painted on a shattered heart.

Parallel Lines

Two lines we are
Never to meet
Though side by side
On the same long street
The same starting point
The same distant gleam
But destined to wander
A parallel dream
The same fire we hold
A yearning unseen
A silent desire
To bridge the space in between
To live a life
Where we could have been

The space stretches vast
An uncrossable sea
A love unspoken
An eternal mystery

We watch our world's turn
Bathed in laughter and light
A constant reminder of something so wrong
That feels so right
A love forever parallel

Lost in night
Like some journeys
Forever without a sight.

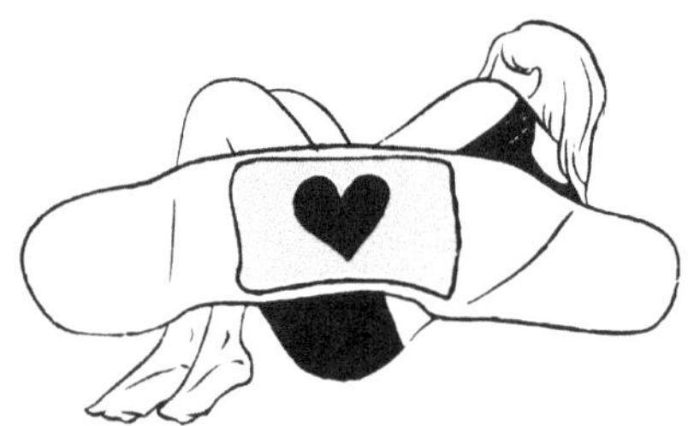

Closure

It tingles,
It burns,
Memories stir,
My heart still turns.

The urge calls,
I pause,
I resist,
Its claws.
A roar within
I silence slow,
With restless chores
To let it go.

Do I reach,
Or turn away?
One small call—
I cannot stay.
I hold the weight,
The quiet strain,
I wear the loss
Like gentle rain.

I retreat,

To hide the ache,
But in the dark,
It starts to break.

I step outside,
Into the day,
Seeking calm
To keep at bay.

It fades,
Though never quite,
But I call it now,
My final fight.

And so I breathe,
The pull, less strong,
And in that breath
I move along.

A letter to self

Broken dreams of a crystal castle
A life of ease
Became a hassle
Life slammed a thunderous crack
The hero vanished
Leaving everything black.
Then the world turned cold
And you had to be bold
Laughter died,
Replaced by screams
Drowning in shadows
U had haunted dreams
Thank you, tiny me
For all the tears you choked
All the prayers
You silently spoke
Thank you
For the rage that burned
To get through it all
For all the lessons learned
For taking care of a shattered soul
For surviving, when hope took its toll.
Can I ever thank you enough?
For walking the paths so hard and rough.
Because of you, tiny broken me

The unknown path, I fiercely see
We walk together, hand in scarred hand
No longer victims, we take a stand
The fire you sparked
Though drowned in tears
Rises defiant
Conquering fears
We will face the future
Head held high
Two wounded souls
That learned to fly.